Kelly's Smelly Wellies

Clive Gifford

Illustrated by Peter Lawson

Kelly was strolling through the grass on Dill Hill.
She had been ill all week with a cold and chill.
Her nose was full of cold and being unwell was dull.

Kelly spotted a large puddle with water as clear as glass.
She thought, "It would be fun to jump in and do a little dance!"

But she was wearing her
best yellow shoes and dress.
It would spell trouble with Mum
if she got in a mess.

Then Kelly spotted a pair of scruffy yellow wellies.

Can you draw a line between the pairs of words which rhyme?

stiff	miss
cuff	hill
loss	spell
smell	ball
will	unless
hiss	boss
hall	whiff
dress	fluff

"Shall I or shall I not?" Kelly asked herself. "Yes, I will!"
She took off her shoes and pulled on the yellow wellies.
Kelly plopped one welly in and giggled at the splash.
Then she jumped into the middle of the puddle and in a flash…

…she yelled,

as the puddle was

a deep well,

so she fell

and fell.

Kelly suddenly stopped.

Where?

She could not tell.

A big man stood over her and said, "Well, well, well. What's this?
I am Sheriff Gruff and I work for Princess Tess."

4

Kelly's word wheel spells out the word **puddle**. Can you work out what the other six word wheels spell? Start with the letter on the blue background.

"You are trespassing on the Princess's lands," said Sheriff Gruff. "What is your name and address?" He was getting tough!

Kelly told Gruff about the wellies and the puddle. Gruff started to scoff and her story came out in a muddle.

"Well, maybe a spell in my cells will help," sneered Gruff. "Then you can tell your story to Princess Tess."

Kelly's legs turned to jelly and she felt very cross. Locked in a cell by a sheriff – what a terrible mess!

Can you follow the list of instructions to create eight different words? You need to fill in each word before you can go on to the next instruction. A clue is that all the words end in **ll**.

1. The opposite of feeling well. _____

2. Change the first letter to make a new word. _____

3. Add a letter to the start to make a round object you can kick and play catch with. _____

4. Change the first letter to describe the opposite of not short. _____

5. Add a letter to the start to make a word for a stand at a fair. _____

6. Change the second letter to describe something that is not big. _____

7. Change a letter to describe what you do with your nose. _____

8. Change a letter to describe a snail's house. _____

Sheriff Gruff led Kelly from her cell to a glass hall.
In the hall sat Princess Tess, who was pretty and tall.
She wore a glass crown, and diamond cuffs on her dress.
"Tell me your story, little lass," said the Princess.

Kelly told her about how
she had jumped in the puddle,
fallen right through
and was now in a muddle.

"We are in a muddle, too, little miss,"
said Princess Tess.
"A bad troll called Pigswill
has caused me much distress."

The lines of this limerick poem are all mixed up. Can you write them out in the correct order?

Than a thin summer dress,

And became ill with a chill, did Jill.

Who, all winter, stood on a hill.

There once was a girl called Jill,

She wore nothing less,

"Pigswill the troll lives in a dell in Chill Hill.
He keeps kissing people and making them ill.
One kiss from a troll and you fall under their spell.
Most people become frogs or seagulls or even seashells!"

As the Princess talked,
others in the hall began to sniff.

Sheriff Gruff said,
"What is that gross **whiff**?"

With the cold in her nose,
Kelly could not tell.
Her wet yellow wellies
had really started to smell!

Many words have more than one meaning. Find a word that fits both meanings.

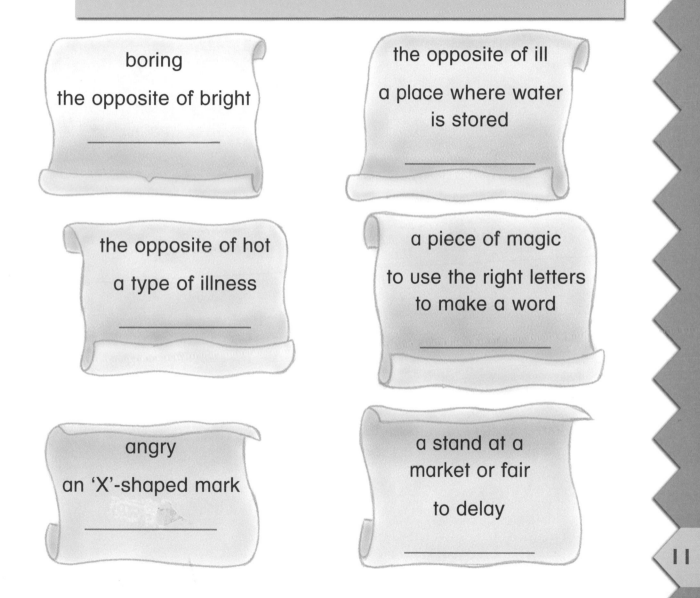

boring

the opposite of bright

_____

the opposite of ill

a place where water is stored

_____

the opposite of hot

a type of illness

_____

a piece of magic

to use the right letters to make a word

_____

angry

an 'X'-shaped mark

_____

a stand at a market or fair

to delay

_____

Kelly's smelly wellies caused much distress in the glass hall. Some people fell over, whilst Princess Tess felt unwell.

Sheriff Gruff put clothes pegs on their noses to stop more falls.

Kelly said sorry for her wellies upsetting them all.

"I have a cold in my nose, so cannot smell well," sniffed Kelly.

"No one likes smelly **riff-raff**," said Sheriff Gruff in a huff.

"Sheriff Gruff, enough! I have an idea," said Princess Tess. "Kelly, will you use your smelly wellies to get us out of a mess?"

Look around the home of Princess Tess on pages 8, 10 and 12 and see if you can answer these questions.

 1. How many trumpeters are there? _____

 2. How many points does the Sheriff's star have? _____

 3. What is the colour of the clothes pegs on everyone's nose? _____

 4. Is the Princess's throne yellow, green or blue? _____

 5. What is the Princess wearing on her head? _____

6. What animal is in front of the Princess's throne? _____

Kelly said, "Yes", she would do what Princess Tess asked.
She ran out of the hall and through Criss-Cross Pass.
On the other side of the pass was Chill Hill.
Kelly was to visit the troll called Pigswill.

Kelly opened the door and crept
into Pigswill's messy dell.
By now her yellow wellies were
giving off a horrible smell.

Even Kelly could sniff
the terrible whiff a bit.
"What a gross pong and whiff
– hope it does the trick!"

Can you add either ll or ff to each set of letters to make a word? Two sets can have either ll or ff, so write both words.

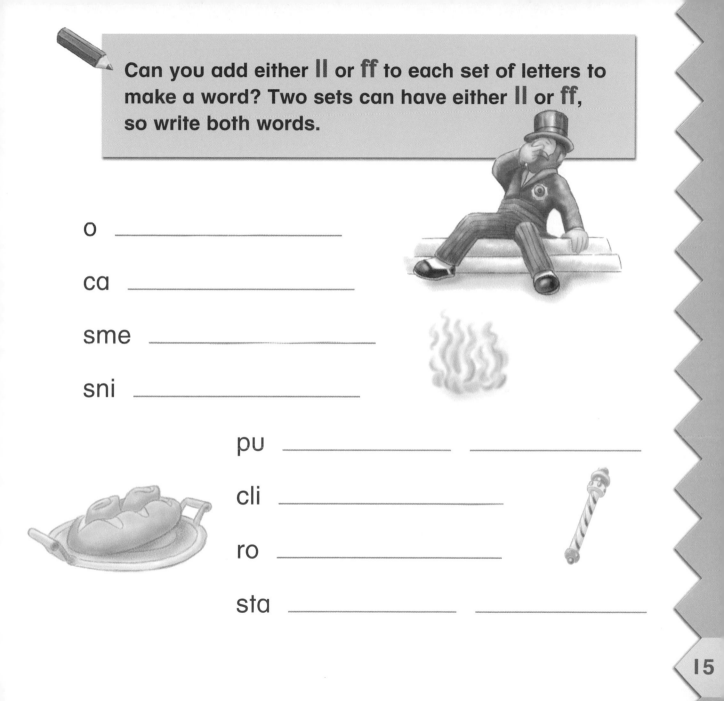

o _____

ca _____

sme _____

sni _____

pu _____ _____

cli _____

ro _____

sta _____ _____

" **M** mm, you must be dinner,"
said Pigswill, looking at Kelly.

"I shall **grill** you,
then **chill** you,
then put you in my **belly**."

"There will be no grilling or chilling,"
Kelly hissed.

"Here, have a smell of
my wellies.
Take a good sniff!"

Pigswill sniffed and cried,
"Ugh! That whiff scares me stiff!"

"Well, the Princess tells me you will not move to a new address,"
Kelly said. "But if you do not go, I'll pull a welly over your head.
The whiff will make you ill and you will be in a mess!"

These are all things found in the land ruled
by Princess Tess. Can you match each word to
a picture?

troll princess cell sheriff throne cliffs well moss

_____ _____ _____ _____

_____ _____ _____ _____

Kelly watched Pigswill flee the lands of Princess Tess.
She skipped back over the pass, happy with her success.

She met Sheriff Gruff,
who was no longer in a huff.
"I am sorry I scoffed –
you showed Pigswill who was **BOSS**!"

He handed her a small glass bell,
a present from the Princess.

"Ring the bell and you will be
back home in a minute or less.
First, please leave your wellies at
Criss-Cross Pass.
The smell will keep the troll away
and we will be free at last!"

An adjective is a word that describes something. All these sentences are missing their adjectives. Can you add the right one to each sentence?

bad   smelly   terrible   deep   messy   little

1. The puddle was a _____ well.

2. Locked in a cell by a sheriff – what a _____ mess!

3. "A _____ troll called Pigswill has caused me much distress."

4. "Tell me your story, _____ lass," said the Princess.

5. Kelly's _____ wellies caused much distress.

6. Kelly opened the door and crept into Pigswill's _____ dell.

Kelly took off her wellies and rang the glass bell.
In a flash, she was back on Dill Hill by the well.

Her bare feet
would not help her chill.
So she found her best yellow shoes,
still on Dill Hill.

As she strolled home, she thought about her day.
Maybe she'd fallen asleep somewhere along the way.
Had it all been a dream?
Something jingled in the pocket of her dress.

Wow! She pulled out the glass bell from Princess Tess!

Now you have read the story of Kelly's Smelly Wellies, try to fill in the gaps in these sentences.

1. Kelly had been ill all _____.

2. She was strolling on _____ Hill.

3. Kelly put on yellow _____ to jump in the puddle.

4. _____ Gruff scoffed at Kelly's story.

5. Kelly was put in a _____ by Sheriff Gruff.

6. The troll lived in a dell in _____ _____.

7. Princess _____ asked Kelly to help her out of a _____.

8. Kelly ran through _____-_____ Pass to get to the troll's home.

9. Kelly found the _____ bell in her _____.

21

Answers

Page 3

stiff – whiff

cuff – fluff

loss – boss

smell – spell

will – hill

hiss – miss

hall – ball

dress – unless

Page 5

across	chills
scruff	spells
smelly	trolls

Page 7

ill	stall
all	small
ball	smell
tall	shell

Page 9

There once was a girl called Jill,

Who, all winter, stood on a hill.

She wore nothing less,

Than a thin summer dress,

And became ill with a chill, did Jill.

Page 11

boring, the opposite of bright – dull

the opposite of ill, a place where water is stored – well

the opposite of hot, a type of illness – cold

a piece of magic, to use the right letters to make a word – spell

angry, an 'X'-shaped mark – cross

a stand at a market or fair, to delay – stall

Page 13

1. two	4. green
2. five	5. a crown
3. brown	6. a cat

Page 15

off

call

smell

sniff

pull, puff

cliff

roll

stall, staff

Page 17

cell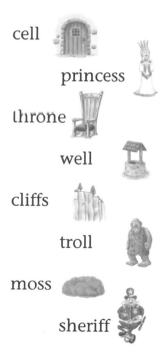

princess

throne

well

cliffs

troll

moss

sheriff

Page 19

1. The puddle was a <u>deep</u> well.
2. Locked in a cell by a sheriff, what a <u>terrible</u> mess!
3. "A <u>bad</u> troll called Pigswill has caused me much distress."
4. "Tell me your story, <u>little</u> lass," said the Princess.
5. Kelly's <u>smelly</u> wellies caused much distress.
6. Kelly opened the door and crept into Pigswill's <u>messy</u> dell.

Page 21

1. Kelly had been ill all <u>week</u>.
2. She was strolling on <u>Dill</u> Hill.
3. Kelly put on yellow <u>wellies</u> to jump in the puddle.
4. <u>Sheriff</u> Gruff scoffed at Kelly's story.
5. Kelly was put in a <u>cell</u> by Sheriff Gruff.
6. The troll lived in a dell in <u>Chill Hill</u>.
7. Princess <u>Tess</u> asked Kelly to help her out of a <u>mess</u>.
8. Kelly ran through <u>Criss-Cross</u> Pass to get to the troll's home.
9. Kelly found the <u>glass</u> bell in her <u>pocket</u>.

Published 2005

Letts Educational, The Chiswick Centre,
414 Chiswick High Road, London W4 5TF
Tel 020 8996 3333   Fax 020 8996 8390
Email mail@lettsed.co.uk
www.letts-education.com

Text, design and illustrations © Letts Educational Ltd 2005

Book Concept, Development and Series Editor:
Helen Jacobs, Publishing Director
Author: Clive Gifford
Book Design: 2idesign Ltd, Cambridge
Illustrations: Peter Lawson, The Bright Agency

Letts Educational Limited is a division of Granada Learning.
Part of Granada plc.

British Library Cataloguing in Publication Data

A CIP record for this book is available from the British Library.

ISBN 1 84315 486 2

Printed in Italy

Colour reproduction by PDQ Digital Media Solutions Ltd, Bungay,
Suffolk NR35 1BY